OF
YORKSHIRE

Front cover picture:
Richmond, The Castle Keep, in 1909

Above:
York, Petergate, 1892

FRANCIS FRITH & HIS UNIQUE ARCHIVE

In 1860, Francis Frith, the Quaker son of a Chesterfield cooper, was 38 years old. He had already sold a massive grocery business he had built up, for a small fortune. Like Livingstone and Stanley, Frith was fired with a romantic wanderlust, and the Victorian deep passion for travelling and exploring. Between 1857 and '59 he made several pioneering photographic journeys to remote regions of the Nile that brought him considerable fame.

After his marriage in 1860, he confined his wanderings a little closer to home and began a series of photo trips around Britain. His aim was to make his pictures available to the greatest number of people possible - life was hard and drab for millions of Victorians, and Frith believed his 'view souvenirs' of seaside resorts, beauty spots and town and village scenes would help keep their rare days out alive in their memories. He was right: by 1890 he had created the largest photographic publishing company in the world!

As well as thousands of views of high streets around Britain, Frith's growing archive included beautiful scenes of leafy glades, dusty lanes, rocks and coastlines, and the boats and riversides, beloved of Victorian wanderers like Jerome K Jerome - whose 'Three Men in a Boat' had struck a strong chord with the public.

Life in the Frith family was never dull. The family went with him on many trips, and the highlights were recorded by his wife, Mary Ann, in her journal. In 1872 she tells of a relaxing three week expedition to Ilfracombe in North Devon. Whilst such trips may have been something of a holiday for his wife and children, Francis Frith found no time to put his feet up. He was up and down the coast photographing Barnstaple and Lynton, hiring carters to carry him out to remote locations, and boatmen to row him round the bay to view and photograph spectacular cliff formations.

After Francis Frith died in 1898 his sons carried on the business for many years with great success, specialising in postcards and other prints. So impressive is the archive he started that **The Financial Times** called it '*a unique and priceless record of English life in the last century*'.

PHOTOGRAPHIC MEMORIES

OF

YORKSHIRE

THE FRANCIS FRITH COLLECTION

This edition published by
The Francis Frith Collection exclusively for
Selecta Books Ltd., Roundway, Devizes,
Wiltshire SN10 2HR
in association with Michael Brewer.

First published 1995

ISBN 1 85937 014 4

Printed in Singapore

The Francis Frith Collection
The Old Rectory, Bimport, Shaftesbury, Dorset SP7 8AT
Tel: 01747 855669 Fax: 01747 855065

Contents

SHEFFIELD, steel capital of Britain, set in the shadow of the Pennines, has been famous for its cutlery since medieval times. Thanks to the inventive genius of Benjamin Huntsman, who discovered how to purify steel through the crucible process, Sheffield expanded rapidly, with fine public buildings and a huge spread of Victorian suburbs to house the fast growing work force.

Right: A horse-drawn tram at Sheffield in 1870. We often think that advertising is a product of our modern society, but Victorian industrial giants like Sunlight Soap were as keen as big companies are today at covering every surface they could, including trams, with brand names.

Above: Fitzalan Square, Sheffield in 1902. A busy square in the heart of the city with the Market Hall in the background. Here the cabs ply for trade, competing with the new electric tram-cars that had begun to thread their way through the city to link the suburbs with the shops and factories. A workman is up a ladder repairing one of the street lamps.

Above: The Crimean Monument, Sheffield, 1893. Here, we are to the south of the city centre, at the junctions of Union Street and South Street, and close by the Empire Palace Theatre. The monument to the Crimean campaign, grand celebration of Britain's imperial splendour, soars proudly over the surrounding buildings. People were probably even fonder of the new public lavatories alongside. In the backgound is the Public Benefit Boot Company.

Left: The Town Hall, Sheffield, 1902. Sheffield was very proud of its majestic new Queen Anne style Town Hall, considered by a contemporary writer as 'a very handsome erection without undue elaboration, and as yet un-smoked' - the city had a reputation as one of the blackest in the country because of smoke pollution from its factories. In the centre is the Jubilee Monument.

Above: Endcliffe Woods, near Sheffield, 1893. A welcome break from the smoke and the grime for three lads and their dog. Sheffield was notable for its open spaces, and here an attractive park has been laid out for the benefit of the local working people, with stepping stones across the stream, rustic seats and ornamental trees.

Left: The Canal Basin, Sheffield, 1870. Close by the Corn Exchange, the canal extended deep into the heart of the city, bringing raw materials to the factories. Here barges have been loaded with scrap metal. On the right a goods train winds its way round to the L & NW goods station and coal yard a few yards away.

Opposite: Fargate, Sheffield, 1893. The Jubilee Monument and the Albany Hotel - a temperance hotel for more sober and upright visitors to the city.

DONCASTER. Standing on a plain watered by the River Don, ringed by mining villages, and in the heart of the Yorkshire coalfield, Doncaster was renowned for its railway works and heavy industries. The classic St Leger race had been run here since 1776. Victorian travellers and pleasure-seekers found the town clean, well-built and prosperous, but with no special attractions to detain them.

Top: High Street, Doncaster, 1903. On the right is the York City and County Bank with its spectacular rustication. Victorian banks went out of their way to impress clients with their premises, often pulling down beautiful old Georgian shopfronts to erect 'grander' new buildings that completely altered the architectural look of the street. **Above: Station Road, Doncaster in 1903**. In the background is the Grand Theatre. Three young boys, on their way home from school, are loafing around in the middle of the main street, and a woman chats to a policeman on the right. It all looks very leisurely. Twenty years later they would have risked being mown down by motorcars.

Above: St Sepulchre Gate, Doncaster, 1903. On the left is Hodgson & Hepworth, 'Ready Money Stores', one of the many chains of shops that spread across the country to supply cheap, mainly imported, goods. They have a new building with Venetian-style windows and decorative brick - very impressive, but see how it breaks the old roof line of the street. Just visible above the roofs in the background is St George's Church, the work of Gilbert Scott, and considered by contemporary Victorian critics to be one of his finest achievements. Its tower, with sixteen crocketed pinnacles, rises majestically to 170 feet.

Left: French Gate, Doncaster, 1903. Just round the corner from St Sepulchre Gate, this is a quieter street of small shops, with the Angel Hotel on the right.

Above: The Race-Course Grandstand, Doncaster, 1903. The famous St Leger, four years older than the Derby, has been run from Doncaster since 1776. The course is out on the London Road at Town Moor. The elegant grandstand was built by John Carr and enlarged early in Queen Victoria's reign. Dickens came to the races in 1857 and was not impressed by the atmosphere. He found the Doncaster racegoers 'horse-mad, betting-mad, drunken-mad, vice-mad'. A contemporary guidebook warns visitors that hotel charges are very high during race week - it is obvious that the Doncaster traders made every penny they could out of the race festivities.

Left: Barges on the canal in 1903. Behind is Gilbert Scott's majestic Parish Church.

Opposite: Baxter Gate in 1903. At the junction of St Sepulchre and High Street.

Top: Conisborough Castle in 1895. Set on a knoll overlooking the River Don, the imposing white keep rises dramatically over the surrounding trees. At its foot nestles the pretty village and canal lock. Sir Walter Scott came here when the Don was still a 'limpid stream'. He was so impressed with the romantic scene that he included the tiny chapel set into one of the buttresses into his novel *Ivanhoe*. The view from the top of the castle tower is spectacular, but Victorian visitors were warned that getting up to it could be 'rather giddy work'. **Above: Conisborough Castle in 1903.**

BRADFORD. This thriving and populous city was at the very heart of Britain's Industrial Revolution, and the centre of the wool trade. A Victorian traveller found it a city consisting 'almost entirely of mills', many of which were doubtless smoke-grimed and polluting. But the city worked hard to offer its citizens other benefits. Bradford was the first to have school medical services, school meals and a municipal hospital. It needed them: it expanded vastly in Victorian times, with a rash of tiny back to back tenements.

Right: Manningham Lane, Bradford in 1897. This important thoroughfare heads westwards out of the city past the Theatre Royal, with its wrought-iron colonnaded front. Workmen are up on ladders repainting the windows. Note the knee bandages on the horse in the foreground.

Above: Darley Street, Bradford, 1897. This bustling cobbled street runs alongside the covered markets, opened in the 1870s. They were among the largest in the country. Half way up the street on the left is a striking sign advertising a spectacle maker. It must have cost a mint. Further on are the Public Library with its special News Room, open until 8pm, and the Art Museum.

Above: The Mechanics' Institute in Market Street, 1897. Below it is Matthews and Brooke's 'Bijou Art Saloon'.

Left: Forster Square, 1903. Forster Square, at the very heart of this great city, has been newly landscaped. A photograph taken five years earlier showed cobbles lapping right up to the foot of the statue to Forster 'the Education King'. In the background is the splendid Post Office, open from seven in the morning to ten at night.

Opposite top: Out on the water, Bradford, 1921. A lazy day off work. Manoeuvring the dinghy in such a tight space must have been a little daunting.

Opposite below: The Band Stand, 1923. Crowds are out enjoying the music in the sunshine.

Right: Town Hall Square, Bradford, 1903.
The city's magnificent Gothic-style Town
Hall was much admired. Built in 1873, it
cost £100,000, and the campanile clock-
tower chimed the hours. In the centre of
the open space outside there is a statue to
Titus Salt, who created the model village
and industrial community of Saltaire.

Below: Market Street, Bradford in 1897. A
policeman stands in the centre of the
cobbled intersection. Further along is
another of Bradford's fine civic buildings -
the Venetian Gothic-style Exchange. Lord
Palmerston laid the foundation stone in
1864.

Opposite: Tyrell Street, Bradford, 1903. A
classic and beautiful photograph of the
street that runs adjacent to Market Street.
There is standing room only on the tram-
car. On the left is Booth & Walker's
opulent china and glass showrooms.

HALIFAX. Set in the foothills of the Pennines, Halifax is spectacularly situated, rising over the Hebble Brook. Irregular and ancient in plan, it is one of the great cloth towns; at its famous Piece Hall, the wool merchants traded, and the weavers sold their 'pieces' or lengths of cloth. It is more notoriously the home of the Yorkshire 'gibbet law', whereby cloth stealers were hanged straight away, without the formality of a trial.

Crown Street, Halifax in 1896. A busy town centre scene. On the left, a young postman stands with his hands in his pockets. Beyond is Smith's umbrella shop, which had just diversified into wedding and birthday presents.

Above: The Town Hall from Corn Market in 1900. There are rough pavement setts and a juddering cobbled road surface. Riding on carts without springs must have almost shaken the spine apart. Note the Town Hall with its extraordinary tower. On the left a boy is selling milk in a churn from his cart.

Top: Halifax's spectacular indoor market in 1896. This huge building was a masterpiece of cast-iron construction. Each trader had his or her own booth, from where they could display their wares, hanging shirts and dresses from hooks and laying out smaller items on the bench. It looks as if they are setting up for the day's trading. **Above: Entrance to market, 1896.**

BINGLEY. Smokestack chimneys, great mills, crowded factory complexes - the town of Bingley, set in the valley of the River Aire and cradled in wooded hills, offers a classic picture of industrial Britain in the nineteenth century.

Right: The Five-Rise Locks at Bingley in 1894. This monument to early engineering prowess lifted boats and barges a full sixty feet. It forms one of the most impressive groups of locks on the Leeds and Liverpool Canal. This important canal linked the textile towns of West Yorkshire with the port of Liverpool, where British-made goods were exported all over the world.

Below: The River Aire at Bingley in 1923. Once one of Yorkshire's fairest streams, the Aire was already by the turn of the century polluted by murky mill refuse and was poisonous to fish.

Above: Bingley from Altar Row in 1894.
Washing hangs out to dry in the yards of
terraced houses. The flight of locks
shown on the previous page can be seen
in this picture.

Left: Main Street, Bingley in 1926.
Bingley here looks like a peaceful
country town. But the tram-car shows that
it is a major industrial wool centre. It
linked the heart of the town with the
mills and factories, transporting workers
from the new residential terraces and
tenements that had begun to fill
Bingley's beautiful valley floor in Queen
Victoria's reign.

LEEDS. Dickens said of Leeds that *'you must like it very much or not at all'*. The great centre for the cloth trade, it also had iron works, brass foundries, chemical and bleaching works, flax mills, leather factories and a multitude of other manufacturing concerns.

It also had vast areas of slum housing - dingy back to back terraces - that made life a miserable and unsavoury affair for thousands of Victorian workers. Yet the city's public buildings were splendid, as the selection shown here confirms.

Top: Yorkshire College, Leeds, 1891. Above: The Town Hall, Leeds in about 1894. This was the handsomest structure of its kind in the north, occupying one side of Victoria Square. Classical in style and with a spectacular flight of steps flanked by stone lions, it was built by a young architect called Cuthbert Brodrick, and opened by Queen Victoria in 1858. They named the square in her honour to commemorate the glory of the event.

Above: The Post Office, Leeds in 1897.
The new Post Office and Revenue Office is on the site of the one of the old cloth halls, known locally as the 'Mixed'. A building of this quality and for this purpose could never be built today. Post Offices in Victorian times were so much grander. The postal system was considered a vital part of the public good, and something that the city and community it served could be proud of - very different from today, when Post Offices are closing down, their work taken over by supermarkets and other high street shops.

Left: The New Medical Hall, Leeds in 1894.

LKLEY. The 'Malvern of the North' is set on the River Wharfe at the edge of the moors. Ilkley is the natural centre for exploring Upper Wharfedale, one of the most beautiful valleys in Yorkshire. In 1850 it was little more than a village, then suddenly gained a reputation as a health resort. Villas, hotels and hydros sprung up almost overnight, and it has never looked back. It has even given Yorkshire its most famous song, warning any young men against courting on the chilly moors "baht 'at" - without a hat. It could be fatal.

Brook Street, Ilkley, 1911. Carriages wait patiently outside the station to pick up another trainload of keen health seekers bound for any of the seven listed local hydros. Treatment at these salubrious establishments could cost from 45/- a week, a lot of money in those days.

The Grove, Ilkley in 1921. The car has just turned the corner from the railway station and is heading off along one the town's broad, leafy streets towards The Spa, a particularly popular hydro. Many believed Ilkley's water did not have the special curative powers of water from other spas like Harrogate. Ilkley water was pure but nothing more. It was the walking, rather than the water, that cured the liver.

Above: Winding path across the Moors, 1914. Moorland walking was not yet the vastly popular activity it is today, partly because of the limited public access decreed by many landowners. In consequence, some visitors found the moors somewhat 'monotonous', stretching out featureless in every direction. A proper rest cure included the taking in of a few spectacular landscape features and odd rock formations - 'singular excrescences' as one writer called them. The Cow and Calf Rocks and the rocky knob of Almias Cliff were particularly popular and well worth the long, breezy walk. Then there were wooded ravines with waterfalls and sun-dappled strolls by the River Wharfe.

Left: Brook Street, Ilkley in 1923. Ilkley's main shopping street with Johnson's fashionable Cafe Royal with its smart striped awnings on the corner.

SKIPTON. Capital of Craven and at the edge of a wild tract of limestone country, Skipton had a reputation as an important gateway to the Dales.

Right: Skipton in 1923. As you walked out of Skipton Station the town would have appeared to be dominated by a huge thread-spinning mill and a jumble of gasometers. Yet Skipton, with its popular Saturday markets, managed to hang on to its country town and agricultural atmosphere.

Below: The High Street and Market Place, Skipton, 1893. A broad, spacious street with the parish church and castle in the distance, at the upper end of the town. On the left is William Mattock's wholesale bakery, and on the cobbles on the right a market area.

Top: Swadford Street, Skipton in 1923. Another leafy shopping street . **Below: High Street, Skipton, 1923.** On the left is the library, with an attractive collection of motor cars parked on the cobbled edging outside. At the far end is the elegant and very stylish white stone War Memorial, commemorating the brave men of Skipton who gave their lives in the Great War. It looks a quiet and peaceful little town - John Wesley felt it was so 'pent up' in its valley that 'you can expect little company from without'. The cars put paid to the seclusion and isolation. It was no more than an hour's drive from Bradford.

Right: Negotiating the stepping stones at Beezley Farm near Ingleton in 1929. Here intrepid walkers could enjoy light refreshments in wooden sheds erected close by the Pecca Falls. The walks in the area were in the hands of a local 'Scenery Company', who in 1902 charged 3d a person.

Below: Ingleton Village, 1890. Although it was described in 1902 as ' a large grey village without interest in itself', Ingleton is positioned at the foot of lofty Ingleborough, the most popular mountain in Yorkshire with climbers. So it became a popular tourist centre. Francis Frith, who has given his name to the world famous archive from which the photographs in this book are drawn, had already set up a stockist in the town for his postcard views. On the left you can see the Frith & Co display board.

Above: Market Day, Settle, in 1921. With its bustling Tuesday market, narrow streets and tiny courtyards, Settle, picturesquely placed on the River Ribble, is a pleasing little town, hemmed in by rugged limestone country. On the right, the picture shows the grand Elizabethan-style Town Hall, built in 1832; in the background is the seventeenth century shambles, with shops under the arched arcade below and living quarters above which are smothered in drying washing. All of Yorkshire seems to have turned up to buy or sell, from farmers' wives offering a few jars of pickle to professional market traders.

Left: Settle from Castleberg in 1895. The Frith photographer has toiled 300 feet up Castleberg Crag lugging his heavy camera equipment to take this stunning panoramic view.

Top: Burton-in-Lonsdale in 1890.
This village of old houses, clustered
on the hillside above the River Greta,
is a few miles from Ingleton. Note the
fine cottage vegetable plot in the
foreground.

**Left: The Meeting of the Waters,
Bolton Abbey, 1888.** Here the waters
of the River Wharfe, divided into
bubbling threads by small islands,
come together again, surging with
renewed force down the sunlit glen
towards Bolton Abbey. All summer
long, carriages plied the riverside
drive from the village, carrying visitors
to the 'Fairy Glen', to enjoy the
cascades of streaming water and
exquisite views.

**Opposite top: Bolton Abbey, about
1870.** Painted by Turner, the romantic
ruins are in a beautiful setting of
woods and meadows by the River
Wharfe. Here, a young lady enjoys a
painting lesson.

**Opposite below: Bolton Abbey, the
Devonshire Arms Hotel, 1909.** One of
the best known hotels in the county.

Right: Kettlewell Village, 1900. The lane to Kettlewell threads its way between greystone walls seven hundred feet up the valley of the Wharfe. In the 1830s, this peaceful and breezy village was a busy market town and had a leadmine and a cotton mill. It was once of greater importance than Grassington. By 1900 it had become a centre for tourists, and a contemporary writer said 'in respect of itself and its inns there is no cleaner village in England'.

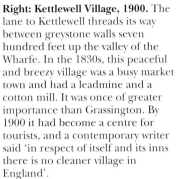

Above: Part of the Square, Grassington, 1926. The grey buildings cluster round the cobbled square. The Post Office on the left is offering a good range of postcards, including some of Frith & Co's. The boys watching the camera on the right must be out on a trip - with their caps, jackets and ties they look far too smart for locals. **Opposite: The Square, Grassington in 1900.** Taken a quarter of a century earlier, you can see the Post Office on the left. The trees that soften the grey stone and cobbles in the later view have not yet been planted. They were probably planted to make the town more attractive for tourists.

Opposite top: A distant prospect of Pateley Bridge in 1893. This pleasant flax-spinning town, with a six hundred year-old market, is perched on the side of a steep hill that rises from the River Nidd. The High Street plunges steeply down to the river.

Opposite below: Pateley Bridge and its churches in 1893.

Above: Burnsall in 1900. A fine Victorian five-arched stone bridge spans the Rver Wharfe. The fells and grassy moors rise all around. You can see the maypole on the village green.

Left: On the river at Burnsall, 1900. A blissful afternoon on the Wharfe. Parasols are up to shade the ladies from the sun. There is no ferryman, so the boat must have been hired by the hour. At the oar is a woman - quite daring in 1900.

ARROGATE. Considered by many to be Yorkshire's most beautiful town, it is set at the gateway to the moors. Stately and dignified, and blessed with curative waters of formidable strength and efficacy, it has long been a celebrated spa town, offering cures for every ailment from gout to nervous tension. Harrogate is a green town, full of trees and flowers - its leafy avenues, shaded gardens and walks make it a paradise for visitors.

Right: Crescent Gardens, Harrogate in 1911. Two elegantly dressed ladies with beautiful hats enjoy the sunshine. In the background, people are hiring chairs and waiting for the awning to come off the bandstand so the music can begin.

Below: Parliament Street, Harrogate in 1907. Horses cantering through the streets of towns were an everyday sight at the turn of the century - there is no other traffic. Note the fine cast-iron colonnade on the left. Harrogate may have been a prim and proper town but there are signs that things are changing - two signs in particular show the inexorable march of the chain stores. The chemist on the left confidently proclaims that his establishment is the largest in the world, and on the right his competitor, Mr Taylor, fights back with a colossal six foot high sign, perhaps proving that size is everything.

Above: Parliament Street, Harrogate. 1923. On the right are the new Royal Baths, opened in 1897, 'in their decoration and roominess unequalled in the kingdom'. For 5/6d you could get a 'mud bath with electricity'. A policeman directs the traffic.

Left: The Pump Room , Harrogate, 1923. This was Mecca for thousands of health seekers. A commentator described the scene in 1902: 'By seven o'clock it is time to be stirring, and from that till the breakfast hour there is a stream - not only of halt and lame, but also of hale and hearty visitors, where bumpers of sulphuric and chalybeate waters are dispensed at the charge of 6d a day. After the first glass a mild constitutional is recommended.'

Top: The Stray, Harrogate, 1902.
This spacious area of grass, intersected
by paths, covered 200 acres, and was
reserved by law in 1770 as a free
unenclosed recreation ground for the
benefit of the people.

**Left: Victoria Square, Harrogate,
1935.** Another of the town's fine
public gardens.

Opposite top: Valley Gardens in 1907.
A small crowd enjoys the antics of a
troupe of clowns. Valley Gardens were
a favourite venue for 'mild
constitutionals' after the taking of the
waters. Set behind the Royal Pump
Room, you could also find the
Magnesia Spring in these gardens,
where you would be charged 1d a
glass.

**Opposite bottom: Station Square,
Harrogate 1921.** Cab fares were a
shilling a mile at the turn of the
century. You could hire a bath chair
for 1s 3d an hour.

KNARESBOROUGH stands on the summit of a rocky hill. Spectacular and picturesque, its buildings clutch the steep sides of the limestone gorge carved by the River Nidd, which is spanned by the magnificent railway viaduct with high arches and embattled parapet. From the river you see flights of steps, overhanging green cliffs and a jumble of gardens and backyards. Knaresborough had England's oldest linen mill and employed cottage weavers from miles around.

The Old Chemist's Shop, Knaresborough, 1911. After two and a half centuries 'the Oldest Chymist's Shop in England' is still dispensing medicines to the people of the town. The apothecary at the time was Mr Lawrence, who ground his potions in a pestle and mortar. Up to 1840 a giant version was turned by dogs in a cage!

Above: Knaresborough from the river in 1921. The great gorge of the Nidd, clothed with wooded banks. **Opposite: Mother Shipton's Inn, Knaresborough in 1914.** Mother Shipton was a prophetess reputedly born in a cave outside the town. Here at the Dropping Well the process of 'petrifaction' could be seen. 'All manner of objects, animate and inanimate, may be seen hardenened into stone - from the savage mongoose to a lady's nightcap - and purchases may be made for a few pence'. The objects were petrified by a trickle of limestone falling like a shower bath. The showroom and workshop were in the Inn.

RIPON. One of the smallest of our cathedral cities, Ripon slopes gently down to the River Ure. On one side of it is the Vale of York and on the other the high moorlands. The photograph on the right shows the spacious oblong market place in 1914. The mighty 90 foot high cross, erected in 1781, is surmounted by a gilded weathervane in the shape of a horn. Charabancs are awaiting their passengers.

Above: The Market, Ripon in 1901. The whole town has turned out to track down a bargain. The streets are jammed tight with carts, wagons and a throng of pedestrians. **Opposite: Fountains Abbey in 1886.** It has been said that Fountains Abbey is unsurpassed in loveliness among the ruins of England, with its soaring tower, great nave arches, beautiful choir and Lady Chapel.

A LDBOROUGH. With its broad village green and delightful mixture of old cottages, Aldborough offers a classic and unchanging picture of old England. But Aldborough draws its fame from its position: the village stands on the foundations of a Roman city, reputedly as splendid as York.

Right: The Green, Aldborough, 1907. In the centre is the striped maypole, and there were stocks and a ruined court-house.

Above: Aldborough in 1907. The tall and ancient stone cross, which is believed to commemorate the Battle of Boroughbridge, is a natural meeting place for village children. The carter pauses for the cameraman before going on to deliver his load of logs. Note how everyone is wearing a hat or cap. You see this time and again in photographs of the period. People must have felt undressed without something on their heads.

Above: High Street, Boroughbridge in 1907. Unfairly described at the time as 'a rather grimy, red-brick and very old-fashioned looking town', it has to be admitted that Boroughbridge probably saw its best days when coaches passed through on the Great North Road. Yet there are fine old houses, historic coaching inns and a cobbled market place with a well that is said to be 250 feet deep. On the right there are some pleasant old shop fronts, including one tiny Georgian frontage with a multitude of windows divided by mullions.

Left: High Street, Boroughbridge in 1907. A quintessentially peaceful scene, where there is time for the horse and rider to stand and stare.

Right: High Street, Wetherby, 1909. A century before this picture was taken, Wetherby's main street would have rung to the sound of stage coaches passing through. A few years after 1909 it would have been a log-jam of streaming traffic on the Great North Road. This picture shows a brief interval of peace. Yet, even in 1909, the motorcar had arrived - the Angel Hotel on the left declares confidently that 'motorists are catered for'.

Below: North Street, Wetherby, 1909. More signs of the times. Ward and Sons were probably smiths before they diversified into cars - they were established in 1868. Now they are the AA agent for Wetherby, carrying out repairs to vehicles and selling cycle and motor tyres and Kodak film. Further down the street is yet another motor engineer selling Michelin tyres. Wetherby was not slow to take what advantage it could of the coming of the car and its position on the great trunk road to the North.

Top: The weir on the River Wharfe at Wetherby, 1909. Here the water wheel on the mill no longer turns, but the water surges over the weir between the wooded banks as it has done for a thousand years. **Below: Market Place, Wetherby in 1909.** Wetherby was described at the turn of the century as 'a town with no interest'. The stone is certainly dark and grey but the laughing children who have turned out for the photographer brighten it up immeasurably.

BOSTON SPA. This compact, neat town had a pump room and saline spring, which was discovered by John Shires in 1744. The town's lovely setting by the River Wharfe makes it a natural centre for visitors.

Top: High Street, Boston Spa, 1893. With its quiet streets with neat railings, elegant villas and wayside trees, Boston Spa radiates an atmosphere of relaxing calm. **Above: High Street, Boston Spa in 1906.** Coaches ground their way the thirteen miles up Wharfedale daily from Leeds. With its growing number of hotels and tea shops, the town welcomed trippers with open arms.

Above: The spa baths at Boston Spa, 1897. Here the River Wharfe flows majestically along a broad and beautiful valley. Trees crowd down to the water.

Left: Clifford Village, 1897. A peaceful village scene just a mile from Boston Spa and even less from the Great North Road. At the end of the street is the fine lofty-towered Norman-style church built earlier in the century.

FILEY. This popular Yorkshire resort was called in 1902 the 'antidote to Scarborough - quiet and select as its big neighbour is rackety and cosmopolitan'. If you were of a contemplative frame of mind, content with sea and sand and a 'fairly early arrival of the daily papers', Filey was the place for you. It was certainly hugely popular with the Victorians and Edwardians, who passed their summer days on the sands between the Brig and Speeton cliffs.

Right: The Promenade, Filey in 1901. A quiet stroll along the promenade enjoying the sea breezes is just what the doctor ordered. In the background some clowns are playing to a small, select audience. On the right is a fisherman.

Above: The Promenade, Filey in 1897. Horse-drawn carriages carry less active holiday makers down onto the sands. On the right are Archibald Ramsden's bathing machines. Bathing machines were considered 'cumbrous and ugly' but a necessary evil. Beyond is the broad sweep of Filey Bay, probably the finest along the Yorkshire coast. Filey Brigg, a mile-long rocky reef, was a favourite with picnickers and geologists digging for fossils.

Top: On Filey Sands, 1927. Back from a trip round the bay, happy holidaymakers save themselves getting wet feet.
Below: The Sands at Filey in 1901. The prospect to the south. There are donkey rides, sand castles to build, clowns - one playing a harp - and no shortage of deckchairs to snooze in. All the women are wearing full length dresses, which must have been both uncomfortable and inconvenient for paddling in the shallows and ambling about the wet sands.

SCARBOROUGH. With its ruined castle, fishing village, working port, spectacular sands, luxurious hotels and terraced gardens, Scarborough has always had something to offer everyone. This town of the 'castled rock' was overrun in the summer by day-trippers, just like Blackpool, but its unique character made it everyone's favourite - including many writers - Anne Brontë often visited the town with her sister Charlotte.

Right: Westborough, Scarborough, 1891. One of the main thoroughfares, connecting the heart of Scarborough with the North Eastern Region railway station. On the right are two horse-drawn water carriers.

Below: Belmont, Scarborough, 1890. An elegant party in top hats looks down over Spa Cliffs to the sea. The Spa is a spa in name only. After a fire destroyed the buildings in 1876, an exotic Turkish-influenced pavilion was built with concert hall, art gallery, theatre and restaurant.

Opposite: Fishing boats in the harbour in 1890. A paddle steamer threads its way gingerly out between the fishing fleet which is waiting for a breeze.

Right: Paddle Steamer, Scarborough, 1890. Here the Comet leaves Vincents Pier for a trip round the headland. From the bay visitors could see the ruins of the castle on the hill and the spectacular cliffs. The pier and lighthouse were reached by a drawbridge. In the background you can see the foreshore.

Below: The Harbour, Scarborough, 1890. Anglers fish off the harbour. In the foreground is a barrel top where they cut up the bait. In the background is the prestigious Grand Hotel, which you could not avoid seeing wherever you were in the town. It was thought handsome but much too overpowering. Here in the harbour there was a persistent fishy odour from the herring boats, which wafted around the town, on occasions a little disagreeable to more sensitive noses.

Top: Foreshore Road, Scarborough, 1890.
In the foreground is a fish market, where trippers could buy gurnard, plaice, flounder and whiting straight off the boats. On the right you can see the lifeboat peeping out from its building, and its slipway in the middle of the picture.

Left: The sands from Spa Gardens, 1890.
If you were short of breath you could take the tramway from the sands back up to the Esplanade. The gradient was about 1 in 3, and the cars were hauled up on steel ropes. The cost was 1d.

ROBIN HOOD'S BAY, sometimes called Bay Town, with its cluster of red-roofed cottages perched precariously on rocky ledges, was a favourite haunt of artists. It is set at the north end of the bay that extends from the cliffs at Ravenscar. The cottages are connected with the cliff top above by tortuous flights of steps and alpine-style passages.

Left: Robin Hood's Bay in 1927.

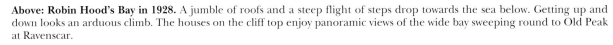

Above: Robin Hood's Bay in 1928. A jumble of roofs and a steep flight of steps drop towards the sea below. Getting up and down looks an arduous climb. The houses on the cliff top enjoy panoramic views of the wide bay sweeping round to Old Peak at Ravenscar.

Above: Robin Hood's Bay in about 1870.
On the shore is a tangle of lobster pots
and fishermen's paraphernalia. A
sailcloth is hanging out to dry. This
unique village has been renowned as a
fishing community since the days of the
early traveller Leland.

**Left: The Shore, Robin Hood's Bay,
1927.** Children paddle in the rock pools
and amongst the dark seaweed. At the
back the cottages teeter on the brink of
the red crumbling cliffs. They have only
very rarely actually fallen into the sea
through erosion. It is said that every
house used to have a hiding place for
smuggled contraband.

WHITBY. A thriving and populous fishing port, with the gaunt clifftop ruin of an ancient abbey. With its bustling narrow streets, the cries of gulls, and fishermen mending their nets on the quayside, Whitby has always exerted a powerful hold over Yorkshiremen. Its chief advantage over Scarborough in the eyes of one contemporary commentator was '*the less mixed character of its clientele*'.

Right: St. Ann's Staith, Whitby, 1886. Near the crossing point of the bridge across the River Esk, this dockside street is in the very heart of Whitby.

Above: The Bridge, Whitby, 1913. A favourite place to stand and stare. The bridge could be raised to allow shipping through. Sterlings' Boot Stores are making a special effort to boost business. **Opposite: Arguments Yard, Whitby in 1913.** A dingy back yard in old Whitby. The boys are barefoot. The cottage on the right is derelict, and the privy door on the left looks fit to collapse. The boys seem happy enough but the future must have looked bleat for many local lads, with the fishing fleet declining fast and a whole way of life coming to an end.

Top: The Fish Quay, Whitby in 1923.
The fishermen stand by their catches
waiting for buyers.

Left: Tin Ghaut, Whitby in 1913. One
of the town's narrow cobbled lanes
leading down to a slipway.

Opposite top: The Quay in 1927. In
the distance are the twin lighthouses
on the East and West Piers.

**Opposite below: Baxtergate, Whitby in
1923.** A bustling shopping street in
the centre of the town, containing the
Post Office, the Angel Hotel and St.
John's Church.

Right: A distant view of Runswick Bay, 1927.
The road winds down through brambles and tangled brushwood down to the village which is set on a sheer cliff. The cottages cling like limpets, some twisted and warped with the effort. In front is the beautiful sweep of Runswick Bay, with a debris of rocks below. The path along the cliff continues through spectacular scenery to Staithes.

Above: Fishing boats with nets drying at Runswick Bay in 1927. There was a tradition with Runswick folk that 'the place where the bairns learned to walk' was on a strip of weed-grown rock and scree set at an angle of about 45 degrees. This prepared them for the seafaring life and for the formidable storms that could batter fishing craft venturing out into the North Sea.

Above: East Row, Sandsend, 1925.
Sandsend was unfortunately dominated by the ugly iron railway bridge in the picture. The line followed the coast for many miles connecting resort with resort. Beneath the bridge, children are sailing model yachts in the tidal streams. The village was also considerably disfigured by a tumble down alum works. Yet the long stretches of sand made it a popular place for family holidays.

Left: Sandsend from above in 1901. New villas are starting to smother the faces of the cliff as Sandsend expands in the only direction it can - inland.

STAITHES. Staithes was to Yorkshire what Polperro was to Cornwall. It once had a huge fishing fleet with hundreds of boats sailing out from the tiny harbour after haddock, cod and mackerel. After the railway came there were weekly fish trains. But as Whitby prospered Staithes declined, and by the turn of the century it was more a picturesque resort than a busy fishing port.

Right: Staithes in 1927. A contemporary description of Staithes says that '*on the shore were bare-legged urchins and dead herrings - with natural result of a fishy odour. Yet for all that there is an air of prosperity about the place,.*

Above: Baiting the lines in about 1890. This interminable and thankless task was very often carried out by the wives and daughters of the fishermen. Down on the shore the butcher's meat and "old clo" were hung up side by side. Yet it was said, '*few tourists will regret delaying their steps awhile to visit this this Elysium of primitive simplicity*". **Opposite: Church Street, Staithes in 1925.** Carrying anything heavy up and down this alpine street made a yoke a sensible aid.

A SKRIGG. A small market town wedged between two hills in Wensleydale. With a long and rich history of local industry - spinning, dyeing, cotton and worsted manufacture, knitting, brewing and lead mining - it was one of the major focuses of life and commerce in Upper Wensleydale.

Right: The River Ure bear Askrigg in 1924. Here the Ure (spelt Yore in some early guidebooks) is a broad placid-looking river, flowing through a wide flat valley. Further downstream, however, it comes swiftly to life, tumbling over a series of cataracts at the celebrated Aysgarth Falls.

Below: The Market Cross, Askrigg in 1911. The scene around the old market cross looks peaceful enough, but in earlier years the whole town would have been a hive of industry. Behind almost every one of the imposing three-storey houses there were dilapidated cottages where the men, women and children lived who laboured long hours at weaving, spinning or mining.

Top: The Post Office, Askrigg, 1911. Askrigg was described in 1902 as a 'dull grey village'. The stone is certainly dark, and apart from the creeper-covered house on the right there are no trees or front gardens to relieve the hardness. Yet it was doubtless a close and friendly community, where neighbour helped neighbour. The Post Office staff have turned out for the photographer. Note the huge arched entrance just beyond. **Below: Farm labourers carrying their scythes, near Askrigg, 1914.**

HAWES. Set on the south side of the Wensleydale valley 800 feet above the sea, this rugged market town once echoed to the sharp clatter of stone quarrying and the rumbling of textile mills. From Hawes, mountain roads wind off into Swaledale, Ribblesdale and Wharfedale, making the town a popular touring centre. It is often called 'T'Hawes' - the 'hause' or pass between the hills.

Right: A distant prospect of Hawes in 1900. Stone walls thread their way across the flanks of the hills behind.

Above: The Holme, Hawes in 1914. A neat and tidy street scene. Here is a great contrast with the rather bleak streets of Askrigg on the previous page. The cottage gardens are bursting with flowers and the whole atmosphere is green and rural. Someone has just bought a new pony and the village postman is making free with his advice.

Top: Market Day in Hawes in 1908.
Left: Market Day in Hawes in 1924.
Hawes obtained its market charter in 1700 and ever since has been the gathering place for farmers from the fells and the hilly lands around. In the 1900s the town was the headquarters of the butter trade for the district. There is very little difference between the two scenes, although separated by sixteen years and The Great War. The farmers' gigs and carts lining the streets are replaced in the later photograph by motor cars and vans. Traders are offering everything under the sun from cloth to china and glass (one dealer has journeyed all the way out from Morecambe). In the autumn the town was filled with Swaledale sheep.

Top: Haymaking at Hawes in 1924. The horse has been led up so that the hay can be loaded onto the sledge.
Above: The School and Village, Hawes in 1900. An untidy street scene, with upturned carts and various heaps of farmers' junk.
Opposite: The Old Mill, Hawes in 1900. Here the wheel is still turning, but in later Frith photographs it has gone. As is the case with so many other small towns, when the industry disappears so does the reason for maintaining the sources of power and other plant.

BAINBRIDGE. The village lies scattered round a neat and pleasant green, shaded by fine old trees. Bainbridge is a settlement with a long history behind it - there are the remains of a Roman fort on Brough Hill.

Right: The Green, Bainbridge in 1929. A delightful cameo of two children pushing their prams across the village green

Below: Bainbridge in 1896. In the centre is the old arched bridge over the Bain, reputedly the shortest river in England. Bainbridge was an important junction: roads radiated out into Swaledale, towards Westmoreland and Lancaster.

Top: The entrance to the village of Bainbridge in 1889. Smoke coils from cottage chimneys.

Left Haymaking at Bainbridge in 1924. It is believed that from ancient times Bainbridge was the home of woodmen working in the great forest of Wensleydale. There is still an unusual custom believed to be associated with this tradition: the 'forest horn' is blown every night at 9pm from the end of September to Shrovetide. No one quite remembers why, but old traditions die hard.

Top: West Burton in 1929. One of Wensleydale's most beautiful villages, its well-kept cottages are grouped round a broad and spacious green. West Burton has always had a reputation as a fashionable place to live, and the shepherd driving his sheep through the village street only adds to its charm. The Black Bull Inn is now a private house.

Left: The Falls at Aysgarth in 1889. The stream pours over a succession of ledges between low, wood-fringed banks. The Falls have dried up completely in the past, but a heavy downpour at the head of Wensleydale soon puts them back into full spate.

Opposite top: Aysgarth Village in 1908. One commentator of the period said 'Aysgarth has no claims for the tourist'. Yet this pretty scene suggests otherwise. Note the gently curving seat for villagers on the right.

Opposite below: Aysgarth Village in 1908. The village became highly popular with visitors to the Falls.

Right: Redmire Village in 1929.
Redmire was once the home of
workers in the Wensleydale coal and
lead mines. The name comes from
the swampy area, now a pond, that
lay near the church. Children play
on the steps of the old cross, long
since gone.

Below: Preston-under-Scar in 1911.
This peaceful village is set below a
massive 'Scar' or crag. In years gone
by, its villagers quarried limestone
for the blast-furnaces of the
steelworks of the North East. By
1914 tourism was the prime
industry.

Top: Carperby, Village and Cross in 1914. Another charming village with a long half-mile street and 17th century market cross.

Left: Carperby, 1914. Children, as usual, have been drawn out by the visit of the Frith photographer to the village. Very often they would follow him around, trying their best to get into every picture he took. It was lucky for us today that they were so persistent, for it is the people that appear in these old photographs that we find so fascinating and captivating, often more than the buildings they lived in.

IDDLEHAM. The fine old castle stands like a sentinel over the village, which occupies the flank of a hill rising from the River Ure. It was once a major market town with seasonal fairs. With its tall grey Georgian houses and ancient Norman keep it has dignity and a long history. Now it is renowned chiefly for the breeding and training of racehorses.

Right: Middleham Market Place in 1896. Charles Kingsley visited the town in 1845. He wrote to his wife, 'Really everyone's kindness here is extreme after the stiff south. The richest spot, it is said, in all England is this beautiful oasis in the mountains'. Praise indeed.

Below: Middleham Market Place in 1926. Photographs of this era always show a considerable 'sprucing up' of village streets compared to those taken in Victorian times. By now, charabancs and motorcars were a common sight in the market place and the village had become a self-conscious tourist spot.

Top: Racehorses at Middleham in 1914. It was said in 1902 that there was 'a decided "horsey" flavour about Middleham society'. In fact, the Middleham stables were famous throughout the land - the all-but-unbeaten 'Flying Dutchman' galloped to success on Middleham Low Moor. The thudding of thoroughbred hooves was a regular feature of Middleham life in the early morning. **Below: Middleham Hall in 1906.** Exercising the hounds.

Right: Bellerby Village in 1929. The village lies on the road that winds from Leyburn to Richmond; a peacful scene with duck pond and broad village street fringed with grass.

Below: Hauxwell Village in 1913. With both parents hard at work in the fields, many young country children had to grow up very quickly. Here three young village girls, dressed in smart white pinafores, look after their younger brothers and sisters. Hauxwell is in the hills to the north-east of Leyburn.

Top: Castle Bolton Village in 1911. Lying high up on a hillside, the village is dwarfed by the massive ruins of its castle.

Left: Gathering the hay at Bolton Castle in 1911. This impressive ruin was called by a contemporary critic 'bare, square and ugly, and from a picturesque point of view it has hardly a redeeming feature'. It can indeed present a dark and forbidding face on stormy winter days, dominating this part of the valley. When the sun is shining and the trees are in full leaf, as in the photograph, it offers a romantic and stirring prospect to visitors and trippers. It was built in the days of Richard II, and in the Civil War was held by Royalists until a diet of horse-flesh forced a surrender. In 1647 it was dismantled. The view from the top is breathtaking.

EYBURN. Commandingly set on a breezy and steep slope, the wind whistles through this attractive market town. It has never been an industrial centre like many other towns of the North Riding. Leyburn is a town of small shops, and a sought-after and fashionable place for the retired; it doubled its population in the first half of the Victorian era.

Right: A street scene in Leyburn in 1911. On stormy days the wind whipped around the streets and squares. You could hardly imagine it from this peaceful scene.

Above: Market Day at Leyburn in 1914. The square begins to fill up with local farmers with their gigs and wagons; shoppers in search of a bargain crowd round the many stalls. The fashionable and prestigious Georgian Bolton Arms Hotel has been the venue for Leyburn Market Club dinners since 1832. The town staged a celebrated and famous October Fair, when the entire market place was filled to bursting with the cries of the auctioneers. **Opposite: The Market Place, Leyburn from the church tower, 1889.**

RICHMOND is one of the most strikingly situated towns in England. A fascinating jumble of broad open spaces and twisting passages, it is guarded by the ruins of a great Norman Castle which looks down on it from a lofty hilltop. Below, in the valley, the River Swale coils and eddies around the town's south face.

Right: Richmond Castle from Bargate Green in 1898. The castle was begun in the 11th century, and after a relentless succession of raids and wars went into decline and disrepair as early as the fourteenth century.

Below: Richmond, Castle and Bridge, 1923. Children play in the shallows of the River Swale. Houses cling to the hillside above, and trees clamber over tops of walls to refresh themselves in the water below.

Top: Richmond, Market Place in 1908. Awnings spread over the rough sloping cobbles. In the foreground is a boot stall with shoes hanging from hooks in swags like grapes. Behind is Richmond's unusual church, which in the 1900s boasted a tobacconist's, a bank, and two butchers as component parts of the building.

Left: Market Place, Richmond in 1923. 'Its buildings are all stone, ye streets are like rocks themselves', wrote the seventeenth century traveller Celia Fiennes about Richmond. The formidable obelisk by the church was erected in 1771.

Above: The Market Place, Richmnond in 1929. Here we have a clear view of some of the shops that were part and parcel of Holy Trinity Church. Lucy Wilcox is selling cigarettes and sweets, and next door is an antique and bric à brac shop.

Left: Richmond in 1929. Across the jumble of roofs and smoking chimneys is the massive 100 foot high castle keep.

Opposite above: Frenchgate, Richmond, 1913. The epitome of a picturesque Yorkshire cobbled street. On the right is the Ship Inn.

Opposite below: The Market Place, Richmond in 1893. In the background is The King's Head Hotel, 'a large and good family and commercial house'.

Opposite: Richmond, the Castle Keep, in 1909. A spectacular view of the steep lane climbing up round the edge of the castle. Horses must have raised sparks from their hooves as they clambered up this precipitous slope hauling a heavy load.

Top: Scorton Village in 1913. A picture of peace and calm, yet the village is only two miles from the Great North road. Like so many other North Yorkshire villages, Scorton has its own broad open green.

Left: Middleton Tyas Village in 1913.

Right: Hipswell Hall in 1913. Close to Catterick Camp, this compact house looks as if it has seen better days. On Hipswell Moor, a thousand feet up, the family would have enjoyed grouse-shooting - the Moor was a renowned preserve.

Below: Hipswell Village in 1913. A neat and tidy village, its cottages hung with creepers, huddling round the central green.

Top: Aiskew Village, 1900.

Left: Catterick Village in 1913. Catterick is a village steeped in history. It was at Catterick in the Dark Ages, says the Venerable Bede, that Paulinus used to baptise his converts in the River Swale, and popular tradition has it that he performed this rite 10,000 times in one day! Catterick is also the site of the battle of Cattraeth between the Britons and the Saxons. Close by the Great North Road, the village is the site of the ancient Roman Station *Caractonium*, which covered nine acres nearby at Thornborough.

N/A

BEDALE. With its cobbled street, wide square and bustling market, this pleasing market town sits astride a long, low hill. Bedale's eighteenth century historian Robert Hird describes his town in fulsome verses as 'the great emporium from whence the Dales were furnished with merchandise'.

Right: Bedale Church in 1896. A shady corner of the town. The church was restored in 1854. The tower had a room on the first floor guarded by a portcullis, suggesting that its use was not always confined to sacred purposes - the Dales were a wild and isolated region in medieval times.

Below: Bedale from the church tower in 1896. From here we see the entire sweep of the broad village street. In the centre is the old cross. A pony and trap passes by too fast for the Frith photographer's camera to capture. On the right, barrels have been laid out ready for collection by the brewer's dray. Awnings are out over the shops on the left, whereas on the right the shops are still swathed in shadow.

Top: Bedale in 1896. Two village lads sit by the village pump with their dog. On the right is the Black Swan. In the background a small crowd is gathering, probably waiting for the carrier's cart to arrive. The trees behind the church form a green and pleasant backdrop to the dusty town street. **Above: The Grammar School, Bedale in 1900.**

ASHAM. With its lovely wide shaded market square and old cross, Masham is an airy and picturesque agricultural town on the edge of the moors. On the main Leyburn to Ripon road, it is the starting off point for excursions to the beautiful abbey ruins of Jervaulx - and for walking trips to the atmospheric moors, where the peace was disturbed only by the cries of birds and the whistling of the wind.

Top: Near Masham in 1936. A gentle stroll on the moors. **Below: The Market Place in 1908**. On the right is the King's Head, recommended as a commodious and pleasing hotel in guide books of the period. The village has recently acquired street lighting - there is a smart new lamp in the centre of the picture, behind which is an animal fold.

Above: Silver Street, Masham, 1908. A workman climbs a ladder outside the Bay Horse Inn. He looks set for a busy day: There are extended ladders all the way down the street.

Left: Roseberry Topping, near Great Ayton, in 1932. This thousand foot summit with its distinctive shape is a landmark for miles around. There were jet mines here - jet is a form of fossilised wood, and was carved extensively at Whitby. Black ornaments and jewellery of jet were immensely popular in the second half of Victoria's reign.

ORK is the historical and cultural capital of the North. With its graceful Minster, ancient walls, twisting medieval streets and historic buildings, it still offers visitors a powerful glimpse of the ancient past. York was especially popular with the Victorians, who had a strong feeling for history and a huge enthusiasm for delving into the monuments and artefacts of the past. Unlike many other town centres, York has survived the ravages of change largely unscathed, as can be seen from these old Frith photographs depicting the very best of the city.

Right: York Minster in 1908. A magnificent prospect of this glorious Gothic building, with its famous Rose window and twin towers. The West front is unequalled in England.

Above: Bootham Bar in 1893. One of the old gateways into the city. The Minster towers over the old city walls.
Opposite: The Shambles in 1909. The jettied buildings hang so far across this narrow market street that neighbours opposite could almost shake hands. Formerly the street of the butchers, the shelves in front of each shop and the hooks overhead were for displaying meat. The smell must have been overwhelming.

Top: Goodram Gate, York in 1892.
A harmonious street of small shops, many medieval in origin. James Todd and his assistant pose stiffly outside his grocer's shop. John Wharton, china and glass seller, stands more casually, hands in pockets.

Left: Bootham Bar, York in 1911.
The walls of the old city date from the 13th century. Bootham Bar incorporates a Norman outer arch, and once had a working portcullis.

Opposite top: York Station in 1909.
The magnificent sweeping curve of the station at York, the railway city of the North. During excavations beneath the platforms, human remains from the Roman period were found.

Opposite below: Lendal Bridge, York, 1909. Here the Ouse is spanned by a bridge built in 1863 to lead travellers to York's first railway station.

Right: The Old Rectory, York in 1909. An exquisite small medieval jettied building with soaring roof and Georgian windows, converted from a Rectory to a shop.

Below: Petergate, York in 1892. This is almost how the city would have looked in medieval times, with the Minster looming mistily over the pantiled roofs. On the right is Merriman the pawnbroker and jeweller's with his impressive illuminated gas lamp. His assistant is displaying the stock. Here we see how sensitive the Victorians could be when they replaced earlier shop fronts, respecting the dimensions of the buildings and the overall look of the street.

Opposite: Stonegate, York in 1886. One of the very finest streets in England. Most of the stone for the Minster was carried up it.

Opposite above: Coney Street, York in 1909. This was one of the city's most fashionable shopping streets. A top-hatted coachman waits outside a dress shop, refusing to acknowledge the driver of the racy new-fangled motorcar parked opposite. Elegant ladies display hats decorated with flowers.

Opposite below: Barges at York in 1886. Here, barges would deliver coal to the wholesale coal merchant. His ramshackle premises, the roof held up on posts, can be seen in the background under the old city walls.

Above: The Cavalry Barracks, York in 1886. The elite of the British Army practice sabre drill. In the background you can see their quarters - they lived above the horses.

Left: Micklegate Bar, York, 1886. Traitors' heads were displayed here in medieval times.

TADCASTER. A bustling market town dominated by lofty brewing chimneys, Tadcaster has been brewing beer since the eighteenth century. The town was an important outpost of the Roman military station at York: traces of coins and pottery were found during excavations, and Roman roads ran all over the town.

Top: Tadcaster in 1901

Above: Bridge Street, Tadcaster in 1907. On the left is a fine old building that looks as if it has seen better days. The signboard above the window says it is 'Ye Olde Tea Rooms'. There is a classic Hovis sign over the first floor and a Fry's chocolate enamel sign at the corner. Opposite are the bright new premises of Becketts Bank.

Above: View from the Bridge at Tadcaster in 1906. A view towards the Mill. Barges plied up and down the River Wharfe delivering to the breweries. The Wharfe was prone to flooding at Tadcaster - the Victorians actually moved a church further up the slope out of reach of the waters! In the distance is the 'virgin viaduct'. Built in 1849, the railway that should have used it was never actually built.

Left: The Mill, Tadcaster in 1906. Note the fine decorative brick work and the elegant cupola on the industrial building behind. The Victorians spent much time and money designing and creating factory and industrial buildings that would be a credit to their towns, and in which they could feel a justifiable civic pride.

SELBY. This celebrated market town is set on the Great North Road, and has one of the most magnificent churches in England. Its ancient abbey was founded over 900 years ago by Benedict of Auxerre, who was instructed in a vision to go to 'Selebaie' in England. As he sailed up the Ouse three swans flew down onto the water where the town now stands. Taking this for a sign he planted a cross and the famous abbey was established.

Right: The Market Place, Selby in 1918. The cross was erected in 1790. Selby was described at the turn of the century as 'a cheerful-looking country town busied to some extent in flax-scutching, rope-making, and boat-building'.

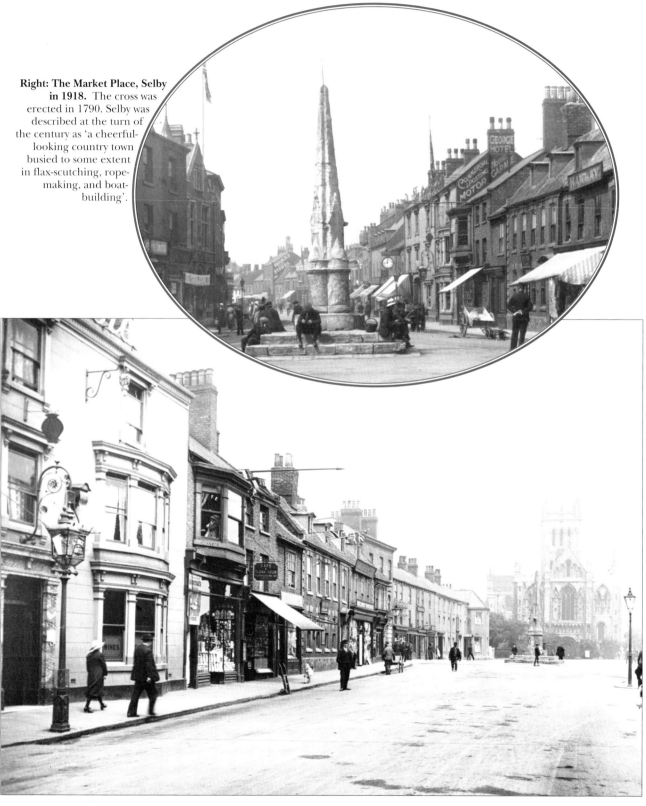

Above: Selby in 1913. Looking towards the broad market place and the beautiful abbey church.
Opposite: The Market Cross and Finkle Street in 1903. In the centre is a branch of Barclay's, then called the York Union Bank. Behind is a street of small shops. It must have been a scorching day - blinds are down and awnings fully extended. Note the little wicker-work hand cart on the left, a common feature of towns at this time.

Above: The Old Toll Bridge at Selby in 1918. An untidy part of the Ouse waterfront. For centuries small boats journeyed up-river to unload at the town's dock.

Left: The Market Place and Abbey Church, Selby in 1936. A tourist coach is out from Leeds. The County roads authority have already started to display the insensitivity that is so common today: directly in front of the old cross they have positioned an ugly road sign. It all looks so much more 'urban' than in earlier views.

Opposite above: Gowthorpe, Selby in 1936. On the left is a famous name from the past - a Raleigh cycle shop.

Opposite below: The Abbey Church, Selby in 1901. Begun in 1100, it became the parish church at the Dissolution, thus avoiding the ruinous fate of other great churches like Fountains Abbey.

Index